50 WAYS WITH

PASTA

50 WAYS WITH

PASTA

KATHARINE BLAKEMORE

CRESCENT BOOKS

NEW YORK • AVENEL, NEW JERSEY

Published by Lansdowne Publishing Pty Ltd
Level 5, 70 George Street, Sydney NSW 2000, Australia

Managing Director: Jane Curry
Production Manager: Sally Stokes
Publishing Manager: Deborah Nixon

First published in 1994

This 1994 edition published by Crescent Books,
distributed by Outlet Book Company, Inc., a Random House Company,
40 Engelhard Avenue, Avenel, New Jersey 07001.

Random House
New York • Toronto • London • Sydney • Auckland

Project Coordinator/Editor: Bronwyn Hilton
Designed by Kathie Baxter Smith
Photography by Andrew Elton
Food Styling by Mary Harris
Recipes typeset in Granjon by Character, North Sydney
Printed in Singapore by Tien Wah Press (Pte) Ltd

National Library of Australia Cataloguing-in-Publication data

Blakemore, Katharine.
50 ways with pasta

Rev. ed.
ISBN 0-517-12058-5

Front cover photograph: Fusilli with Fresh Tomato, Mozzarella and Basil Sauce, recipe page 38
Page 2: Farfalle with Watercress, Avocado and Pistachios, recipe page 30
Pages 8 & 9: Noodle and Seafood Casserole, recipe page 50
Back cover photograph: Tuna-stuffed Cannelloni, recipe page 102

CONTENTS

Introduction 6
The Recipes 9

INTRODUCTION

Pasta originated in Italy, and is now one of the world's favorite foods. Shop and supermarket shelves worldwide are stocked with countless varieties of pasta in many shapes and sizes, and makers of fresh pasta in different countries reproduce most of the regional styles of Italy, from the tiny orecchieti of Apulia to the ribbon-like tagliatelle of Bologna. Pasta can be served simply with a herb-flavored butter, or enhanced by an elaborate sauce; it can be plain, or filled with spiced mincemeat; it can be made from wholemeal flour, or incorporate spinach or tomato, to add a decorative green and orange to the dish. In all these ways, pasta makes a fine first or main course and even, surprisingly, a delicious dessert.

Pasta is most readily available dried, and is made either from durum wheat flour alone, or flour with the addition of egg. In this form it will keep many months before cooking. Fresh pasta, including the filled shapes such as ravioli or tortellini, can be bought vacuum-packed, or from chilled cabinets, in which case it should be kept in a refrigerator, for no more than a few days. Fresh pasta can also be frozen successfully, and takes considerably less time to cook than dried pasta. A simple recipe for fresh pasta is included on page 110 of this book.

To cook any of the pastas mentioned in this book, heat a large enough quantity of water for the pieces to move about freely without sticking together, bring the water to the boil, and add a little salt if desired. Add the pasta and bring back to the boil, then cook uncovered over a fairly high heat, stirring occasionally with a wooden spoon or fork. Bought pasta usually has a cooking time indicated on the packet, but the best way to test pasta is by biting into it: when it is cooked it should be firm but not hard. If it is overcooked, it becomes soft and sticky. Pasta which will be recooked in another dish (such as lasagne) should be just undercooked in the water. Drain the pasta well before serving.

Pasta can be served with a variety of sauces, to suit individual preferences concerning meat, vegetables and taste. The accompaniments in this book are designed to be light and healthy, and the small amount of fat used to cook these sauces can be further reduced if non-stick utensils are used.

Particular pasta shapes have been specified for each of the recipes, but in many cases they are interchangeable. Parmesan cheese is a traditional accompaniment to many pasta dishes: buy it fresh in a piece whenever possible, and grate it just before serving.

As pasta is such a versatile food, this book contains recipes for soups, main-course dishes that can be halved to make starters, and even recipes for desserts. Included with the individual recipes are instructions for microwave cooking where relevant.

Types of Pasta

Amori: pasta twists

Bucatini: thick spaghetti

Capellini: angel hair pasta

Conchiglie: shell pasta

Farfalle: pasta bows

Fettucini: ribbon pasta

Fiochetti: (also called farfallini) tiny butterfly-shaped pasta with serrated edges

Fusilli: pasta twists

Orecchieti: ear-shaped pasta

Paglia e Fieno: green and white tagliatelle

Pastini: very small pasta shapes

Penne: pasta quills

Pipe Rigate: ridged bent pasta tubes

Rigatoni: ridged pasta tubes

Spaghettini: flat spaghetti

Tagliatelle: ribbon pasta

Tortellini: small filled pasta rounds

Tortiglioni: diagonally-ridged pasta tubes

Trenette: long thin strips of pasta with square cut edges

The Recipes

ANELLI WITH LEEKS AND HAM

1 oz (25 g) butter
1 lb (500 g) leeks, sliced
8 oz (250 g) raw gammon (bacon)
or ham, diced
1 oz (25 g) flour
1 cup (8 fl oz, 250 ml) light stock
¼ cup (2 fl oz, 50 ml) dry white
wine
¼ cup (2 fl oz, 50 ml) light
(single) cream
12 oz (350 g) anelli (pasta rings)
salt and freshly ground black
pepper
freshly grated parmesan cheese

Melt butter in a large pan, add leeks and gammon and cook gently for 5 minutes until leeks are beginning to soften.

Stir flour into the pan, cook for 1 minute then add stock, wine and cream. Bring to the boil, stirring constantly, then cover the pan and simmer gently for 10 minutes, stirring from time to time.

Cook anelli in boiling salted water for 5 to 8 minutes, drain well, then add to the sauce.

Taste and adjust seasoning, then divide among four warmed plates. Serve sprinkled with parmesan cheese.

Preparation time 10 minutes
Cooking time 20 minutes
Serves 4

BAKED PASTA WITH SMOKED FISH

1 lb (500 g) smoked haddock or
cod fillet
1 onion, chopped
2 sticks celery, sliced
8 oz (250 g) green and white
fusilli
1 tablespoon cornstarch
(cornflour)
1 cup (8 fl oz, 250 ml) milk
2 hard cooked eggs, chopped
1 tablespoon chopped fresh parsley
salt and freshly ground black
pepper
1 cup (2 oz, 50 g) fresh brown
breadcrumbs
¼ cup (1 oz, 25 g) cheddar cheese,
grated

Put fish, onion and celery into a pan, cover with cold water, bring just up to boiling point, cover pan, remove from heat and let stand for 10 minutes. Drain, reserving 1 cup (8 fl oz, 250 ml) cooking water (stock).

Cook pasta in boiling water for 5 to 8 minutes until still quite firm.

Mix the cornstarch with a little of the milk, mix the remaining milk with the fish stock, put into a large pan, add the cornstarch, heat gently, stirring constantly until mixture thickens then cook for 2 to 3 minutes. Remove from the heat.

Flake fish and add to the pan with celery, onion, pasta, eggs and parsley. Taste and adjust seasoning. Pour into an ovenproof casserole.

Mix together the breadcrumbs and cheese, sprinkle over the top of the casserole. Cook in a preheated oven 400°F (200°C, Gas mark 6) for about 30 minutes until breadcrumbs are crisp and brown, or microwave 6 to 7 minutes on HIGH.

Preparation time 15 minutes
Cooking time 45 minutes
Serves 4

Microwave tip: If cooking this dish in the microwave, finish off under the broiler (grill) to brown the breadcrumbs.

BEAN AND PASTA SOUP

1 onion, sliced
3 sticks celery, sliced
*4 slices smoked streaky bacon,
    rinded and chopped*
1 tablespoon olive oil
*5 cups (2 pints, 1.2 liters) beef
    stock*
*1 cup (6 oz, 175 g) cooked or
    canned black-eye beans*
*1 cup (6 oz, 175 g) cooked or
    canned lima (butter) beans*
3 oz (75 g) pipe rigate
*salt and freshly ground black
    pepper*

Fry onion, celery and bacon in oil in large pan for 2 to 3 minutes.

Add stock and beans, bring to the boil, cover the pan and simmer for 30 minutes.

Add pasta to the pan, cook for a further 10 to 15 minutes until pasta is tender, season to taste.

Preparation time 10 minutes
Cooking time 45 to 50 minutes
Serves 4 to 6

Variation: Try using other beans such as cannellini, borlotti or red kidney beans or a combination of three or four.

BEEF TERIYAKI
WITH BUCKWHEAT NOODLES

10 oz (315 g) buckwheat) (soba)
    noodles
salt and freshly ground black
    pepper
1–2 tablespoons vegetable oil
1¼ lb (550g) rump steak, cut into
    thin strips
1 onion, finely chopped
1 clove garlic, crushed
1 tablespoon grated fresh ginger
1 teaspoon ground cumin
½ teaspoon coriander seeds,
    crushed
1 stalk lemon grass, finely chopped
1 tablespoon miso
1 cup (8 fl oz, 250 ml) beef stock
1 tablespoon soft brown sugar
2 teaspoons cornstarch (cornflour)

Cook the noodles in boiling water for 10 to 12 minutes.

Heat 1 tablespoon oil in a large non-stick pan or wok, quickly fry the beef until brown. Remove beef from the pan.

Add onion, garlic and ginger to the pan, adding a little more oil if necessary. Cook for 2 to 3 minutes then add cumin, coriander seeds and lemon grass.

Mix together the miso, stock, sugar and cornstarch. Add to the pan, bring to the boil, stirring constantly, then replace beef. Simmer gently until beef is heated through. Season to taste.

Drain the noodles, divide among four warmed plates. Divide the beef among the plates of noodles.

Preparation time 20 minutes
Cooking time 15 minutes
Serves 4

Note: Teriyaki is a Japanese dish consisting of meat, chicken or seafood, marinated in a mixture of soya sauce and mirin. It is basted with marinade or glaze while cooking and this produces a golden colour with a mild, delicate, sweet taste.

CHICKEN NOODLE SOUP WITH EGG

*8 oz (250 g) carrots, cut into tiny
   cubes*
8 oz (250 g) leeks, thinly sliced
*5 cups (2 pints, 1.2 liters) chicken
   stock*
*4 oz (125 g) cooked chicken,
   shredded*
2 oz (50 g) vermicelli
2 eggs
juice of ½ lemon
freshly ground black pepper

Put the carrots and leeks into a large pan with the stock, bring to the boil, reduce heat, cover the pan and simmer for 10 minutes.

Add the chicken and vermicelli to the pan and cook for a further 5 minutes.

Mix the eggs with the lemon juice, add ½ cup (4 fl oz, 125 ml) stock from the pan, mix well then strain back into the pan. Reheat gently, stirring constantly, but do not allow the soup to boil. Taste and adjust seasoning.

Preparation time 10 minutes
Cooking time 20 minutes
Serves 4

Variation: When serving this very nourishing soup to children try using alphabet or animal pasta shapes.

Note: Use the carcass of a previously cooked chicken to make the stock. Retain a little of the chicken meat to add to the soup.

CHINESE-STYLE PORK WITH FRIED NOODLES

8 oz (250 g) Chinese egg noodles
salt and freshly ground black
  pepper
1–2 tablespoons sunflower oil
1 tablespoon sesame oil
12 oz (350 g) lean pork tenderloin
  (fillet), thinly sliced
1 bunch scallions (green onions,
  spring onions), sliced
1 small piece of fresh ginger, cut
  into thin matchsticks
6 oz (175 g) mushrooms, sliced
6 oz (175 g) beansprouts
2 tablespoons soy sauce
½ cup (4 fl oz, 125 ml) light stock
½ teaspoon five-spice powder
1 teaspoon cornstarch (cornflour)

Put the noodles into a pan of boiling salted water, cover pan and let stand for 5 minutes. Drain well then dry on paper towels.

Heat 1 tablespoon sunflower oil and the sesame oil in a large non-stick pan or wok. Fry the noodles until lightly browned, then transfer to a serving dish and keep warm.

Add the pork to the pan, adding a little more sunflower oil if necessary. Stir-fry until brown.

Add the scallions, ginger, mushrooms and beansprouts. Cook for a further 2 to 3 minutes.

Mix together the soy sauce, stock, five-spice powder and cornstarch. Add to the pan, bring to the boil, stirring constantly. Taste and adjust seasoning. Pour over noodles and serve immediately.

Preparation time 20 minutes
Cooking time 10 minutes
Serves 4
Note: This dish could be made with some leftover roast pork. This will not need to be stir-fried.

CONCHIGLIE WITH BROCCOLI, LEMON AND ALMONDS

1 lb (500 g) conchiglie
salt and freshly ground black
 pepper
1 lb (500 g) broccoli florets
½ oz (15 g) butter or margarine
1 oz (25 g) flour
1 cup (8 fl oz, 250 ml) chicken
 stock
2 tablespoons heavy (double)
 cream
grated rind and juice of ½ lemon
¼ cup (1 oz, 25 g) flaked almonds,
 toasted
lemon wedges

Cook pasta in boiling salted water for 7 to 8 minutes. Add broccoli to the pan and cook for a further 5 minutes.

Melt butter in another pan, add flour, mix well then cook for 1 minute. Gradually add chicken stock and bring to the boil stirring constantly. Cook for 2 minutes then add cream, lemon rind and juice. Taste and adjust seasoning.

Drain pasta and broccoli, transfer to a warmed serving dish. Pour the sauce over the pasta, sprinkle with the almonds and garnish with the lemon wedges.

Preparation time 10 minutes
Cooking time 15 minutes
Serves 4
Note: If serving this dish to a vegetarian, omit the chicken stock and use a vegetable stock instead.

COTTAGE CHEESE
WITH VERMICELLI FRITTERS

6 oz (175 g) cooked vermicelli
2 cups (1 lb, 500 g) cottage cheese
3 eggs, separated
3 tablespoons chopped fresh chives
1 bunch scallions (green onions,
*   spring onions), finely chopped*
1 oz (25 g) flour
salt and freshly ground black
*   pepper*
1–2 tablespoons vegetable oil

Mix the vermicelli with the cottage cheese, egg yolks, chives, scallions, flour, salt and pepper.

Whisk the egg whites until stiff then fold lightly into the cottage cheese mixture.

Brush the base of a large non-stick pan with a little of the oil. Drop tablespoonfuls of the mixture into the pan, cook until the undersides are brown, then turn and brown the other side. Drain very well on paper towels.

Keep warm in a low oven while cooking the remainder of the mixture in the same way.

Preparation time 10 minutes
Cooking time 10 minutes
Serves 4

COUNTRY VEGETABLE SOUP WITH PASTA

1 onion, chopped
1 clove garlic, crushed
1 large leek, sliced
1 tablespoon olive oil
2 medium carrots, sliced
5 cups (2 pints, 1.2 liters)
*   vegetable stock*
14 oz (400 g) can chopped
*   tomatoes*
2 medium zucchini (courgettes),
*   sliced*
6 oz (175 g) cabbage, shredded
4 oz (125 g) green beans, ends
*   removed*
4 oz (125 g) macaroni
salt and freshly ground black
*   pepper*
¼ cup (4 fl oz, 125 ml) pesto

Soften the onion, garlic and leek in the oil in a large covered pan. Add the carrots, stock and tomatoes with juice from the can. Bring to the boil, cover and simmer for 30 minutes.

Add zucchini, cabbage, beans and macaroni to the pan, season to taste. Simmer covered for a further 10 to 15 minutes until the macaroni is tender.

Divide the soup among six individual bowls. Divide the pesto among the bowls of soup.

Preparation time 20 minutes
Cooking time 40 to 45 minutes
Serves 6

Note: This is a very substantial soup and served with some bread and cheese would make an ideal lunch or supper dish.

EGGPLANT (AUBERGINE) PASTA RING

1 onion, chopped
1 carrot, finely chopped
1 stick celery, finely chopped
1 tablespoon olive oil
1 lb (500 g) lean ground (minced)
  lamb
1 teaspoon ground cumin
1/2 teaspoon ground cinnamon
4 tomatoes, skinned and chopped
1 1/4 cups (1/2 pint, 300 ml) lamb
  stock
salt and freshly ground black
  pepper
1 large eggplant (aubergine)
  thinly sliced
vegetable oil for greasing
8 oz (250 g) cooked bucatini, cut
  into shorter lengths
1 egg, beaten

Cook onion, carrot and celery in oil until soft. Add lamb, stir well then cook until lamb is no longer pink.

Stir in cumin and cinnamon, then add tomatoes, stock, salt and pepper. Bring to the boil, reduce heat, then simmer uncovered for about 30 minutes, stirring occasionally until all the stock has evaporated.

Cook the eggplant slices in boiling salted water for 2 minutes, drain. Dry on paper towels, then lay them in overlapping slices around the inside of a lightly greased 5 cup (2 pint, 1.2 liter) capacity ring mold.

Mix together the meat sauce, pasta and egg. Fill the ring mold with the mixture. Place any remaining eggplant slices on top.

Cover the top of the ring mold with foil, cook in a preheated oven 400°F (200°C, Gas mark 6) for 40 minutes, or microwave in a non-metal container. Cover first with microwave-safe plastic wrap, pierced in a few places, then cook for about 15 minutes on MEDIUM. Turn out onto a warmed serving plate to serve.

Preparation time 20 minutes
Cooking time 1 1/4 hours
Serves 4

FARFALLE WITH WATERCRESS, AVOCADO AND PISTACHIOS

12 oz (350 g) farfalle
salt and freshly ground black
  pepper
½ oz (15 g) butter
1 bunch watercress, stalks removed
2 large ripe avocados, peeled and
  stoned
1 tablespoon lemon juice
1 cup (8 oz, 250 g) fromage frais
½ cup (2 oz, 50 g) shelled
  pistachio nuts

Cook farfalle in boiling salted water for 10 to 12 minutes.

Melt butter in a large pan, add watercress, stir around until wilted then cook for 2 to 3 minutes.

Mash one of the avocados with the lemon juice and fromage frais, add to the watercress, heat gently stirring constantly.

Drain pasta, add to the avocado sauce, mix well then taste and adjust seasoning. Remove pan from the heat.

Cut the remaining avocado into cubes, add it to the pasta with the pistachios. Mix gently then divide among four warmed plates. Serve immediately.

Preparation time 10 minutes
Cooking time 15 minutes
Serves 4

Watchpoint: Heat the sauce very gently. Do not allow to boil as the mixture may separate.

Fettucini Salad
with Beans and Fetta

8 oz (250 g) green fettucini
2 tablespoons olive oil
1 clove garlic, crushed
4 oz (125 g) French beans, halved
15 oz (425 g) can red kidney
    beans, drained
1 green bell pepper (capsicum),
    chopped
6 oz (175 g) fetta cheese, cubed
1 tablespoon tarragon vinegar
salt and freshly ground black
    pepper

Cook the fettucini in boiling water for about 10 minutes. Drain well, transfer to a large bowl, add the olive oil and garlic, toss together then let stand until cold.

Cook the French beans for 5 minutes, drain and cool under running cold water.

Add the French beans, red beans, green bell pepper, fetta cheese and vinegar to the cooled fettucini. Mix gently but thoroughly. Season to taste with salt and pepper.

Preparation time 15 minutes, plus standing time
Cooking time 10 minutes
Serves 4

Variation: Any other fresh or canned beans could be used, according to season and availability.

Watchpoint: Do not add too much salt as fetta cheese can sometimes be a little salty.

FIOCHETTI WITH ZUCCHINI (COURGETTES)

12 oz (350 g) fiochetti
salt and freshly ground black
    pepper
1 onion, chopped
1 clove garlic, crushed
1 oz (25 g) butter
1 lb (500 g) zucchini (courgettes),
    grated
¾ cup (6 oz, 175 g) ricotta cheese
½ cup (2 oz, 50 g) cheddar cheese,
    grated

Cook fiochetti in boiling salted water for about 10 minutes.

In a pan soften the onion and garlic in butter, add the zucchini and cook for a further 2 minutes. Add the ricotta cheese, salt and pepper to the pan, heat gently, stirring constantly.

Drain the pasta, mix with the zucchini sauce, transfer to an ovenproof dish.

Sprinkle with the cheddar cheese, broil (grill) for 2 to 3 minutes until cheese topping is brown and bubbling.

Preparation time 10 minutes
Cooking time 15 minutes
Serves 4

Variation: If ricotta cheese is not available this dish could be made with curd or cottage cheese.

Fresh Tagliatelle
with Herbed Cream Sauce

8 oz (250 g) fresh spinach
  tagliatelle
8 oz (250 g) fresh egg tagliatelle
salt and freshly ground black
  pepper
¾ cup (6 oz, 175 g) low-fat soft
  cheese with garlic and herbs
½ cup (4 fl oz, 125 ml) skimmed
  milk
¼ cup (1 oz, 25 g) parmesan
  cheese, finely grated
2 tablespoons chopped fresh chives

Cook the pasta in two separate pans of boiling salted water for about 5 minutes each.

Put the soft cheese, milk and parmesan into a small non-stick pan, heat gently, stirring constantly to make a smooth sauce.

Drain the pastas, then arrange the spinach pasta around the outer edge of a warmed serving dish. Put the egg pasta in the center.

Season the sauce with salt and pepper, then drizzle the sauce over the pasta. Sprinkle with the chopped chives.

Preparation time 10 minutes
Cooking time 5 minutes
Serves 4

Fusilli with Fresh Tomato, Mozzarella and Basil Sauce

12 oz (350 g) mixed red, white and green fusilli
salt and freshly ground black pepper
4 large tomatoes, chopped
8 oz (250 g) mozzarella cheese, cubed
2 tablespoons fresh basil leaves
¼ cup (2 fl oz, 50 ml) olive oil

Cook the pasta in boiling salted water for about 10 minutes.

Mix together the tomatoes, mozzarella, basil, salt, pepper and olive oil in a large bowl.

Drain the pasta, add to the bowl, toss well, then immediately divide among four warmed plates.

Preparation time 10 minutes
Cooking time 10 minutes
Serves 4

Variation: This dish makes a delicious salad if left to become cold.

FUSILLI WITH WALNUT
AND CORIANDER PESTO

1 lb (500 g) fusilli
½ cup (4 oz, 125 g) crème fraîche
1 tablespoon olive oil
½ cup (2 oz, 50 g) cheddar cheese,
* finely grated*
¼ cup (1 oz, 25 g) pecorino
* cheese, finely grated*
1 cup (4 oz, 125 g) walnuts, very
* finely chopped*
1 large bunch fresh coriander,
* finely chopped*
salt and freshly ground black
* pepper*

Cook the pasta twists in boiling water for about 10 minutes.

Put the crème fraîche into a bowl, add the oil, cheeses, walnuts, coriander, salt and pepper. Mix well until amalgamated or, alternatively, put the ingredients into a food processor and blend until a smooth paste is formed.

Drain the pasta and place into a warmed serving bowl. Add the sauce, mix quickly but thoroughly until the pasta is coated with the sauce. Serve immediately.

Preparation time 10 minutes
Cooking time 10 minutes
Serves 4

Advance preparation: The walnut and coriander 'pesto' sauce will keep for 2 to 3 days in a covered container in the refrigerator.

LEMON PASTA CHEESECAKE

2 cups (1 lb, 500 g) curd cheese
¾ cup (6 oz, 175 g) superfine
  (caster) sugar
grated rind and juice of 3 lemons
3 eggs, beaten
⅔ cup (5 fl oz, 150 ml) sour
  cream
8 oz (250 g) cooked capellini
½ cup (4 fl oz, 125 ml) fromage
  frais
twists of lemon to decorate

Beat together the curd cheese, sugar, lemon rind and juice, eggs and sour cream. Lightly fold in the capellini, then pour the mixture into an 8 inch (20 cm) cake pan lined with non-stick silicone paper.

Bake in a preheated oven 350°F (180°C, Gas mark 4) for about 1 hour until firm to the touch. Remove pan from the oven, let stand until cold.

Remove cheesecake from the pan, peel off the lining paper, place on a serving plate. Spread the fromage frais over the top of the cheesecake and decorate with the twists of lemon.

Preparation time 15 minutes
Cooking time 1 hour
Serves 6

Health tip: Use low-fat soft cheese and unflavored yogurt instead of the curd cheese and sour cream to reduce the fat content of this cake.

Variation: Oranges may be used instead of lemons. If so, reduce the amount of sugar to ½ cup (4 oz, 125 g).

MACARONI CHEESE RING
WITH SAGE

8 oz (250 g) macaroni
salt and freshly ground black
  pepper
1 small cauliflower, cut into
  florets
1 cup (8 oz, 250 g) fromage frais
½ cup (2 oz, 50 g) cheddar cheese,
  grated
pinch English mustard powder
3 eggs, beaten
pinch dried sage
butter or vegetable oil, for
  greasing
8 fresh sage leaves

Cook the macaroni in boiling salted water for 5 minutes, add the cauliflower to the pan and cook for a further 5 minutes.

Mix together the fromage frais, cheddar cheese, mustard powder, eggs and dried sage. Season to taste.

Drain the macaroni and cauliflower, add to the cheese mixture and mix well.

Grease a 5 cup (2 pint, 1.2 liter) capacity ring mold, non-stick if possible, and arrange the sage leaves around the base. Spoon in the macaroni mixture.

Put the mold into a roasting pan half-filled with boiling water. Cook in a preheated oven 375°F (190°C, Gas mark 5) for 35 to 40 minutes until set.

Remove from the roasting pan. Let stand for a few minutes before turning out onto a warmed serving plate.

Preparation time 15 minutes
Cooking time 50 minutes
Serves 4

Variation: Instead of the cauliflower, use a mixture of leftover cooked vegetables in this dish.

MINTY LAMB LASAGNE

1 onion, finely chopped
1 clove garlic, crushed
2 teaspoons vegetable oil
1 lb (500 g) lean ground (minced)
  lamb
2 tablespoons chopped fresh mint
  or 1 tablespoon dried mint
salt and freshly ground black
  pepper
14 oz (400 g) can tomatoes in
  juice
7 oz (200 g) lasagne
1¼ cups (½ pint, 300 ml)
  skimmed milk
1 oz (25 g) flour
½ oz (15 g) sunflower margarine
1 oz (25 g) freshly grated
  parmesan cheese
mint leaves, to garnish

Cook onion and garlic in oil until soft, add lamb to the pan and stir around until lamb is no longer pink.

Add mint, salt, pepper and tomatoes and juice from can. Bring to the boil, reduce heat, cover the pan and simmer for 30 minutes.

Cook lasagne in boiling salted water until just tender. Drain then let stand on paper towels until cool.

Put milk, flour and margarine into a small pan, heat gently, beating constantly until a thick sauce is formed. Season to taste.

Lightly grease a rectangular baking dish. Lay in ⅓ lasagne sheets. Add half the meat sauce. Repeat layers ending with a final layer of lasagne.

Spread the white sauce over the lasagne. Sprinkle with parmesan cheese, cook in a preheated oven 350°F (180°C, Gas mark 4) for 40 minutes, or microwave 8 to 10 minutes on HIGH.

Preparation time 20 minutes
Cooking time 1 hour 10 minutes
Serves 4

MOZZARELLA MEAT BALLS
AND SPAGHETTI

1 lb (500 g) lean ground (minced) beef
1 cup (2 oz, 50 g) fresh white breadcrumbs
1 clove garlic, crushed
2 tablespoons chopped fresh parsley
salt and freshly ground black pepper
1 egg, beaten
5 oz (150 g) mozzarella cheese
1 tablespoon vegetable oil
1 onion, chopped
14 oz (400 g) can chopped tomatoes
12 oz (350 g) spaghetti

Put the beef, breadcrumbs, garlic, half the parsley, salt and pepper into a bowl. Add the egg and mix well.

Cut the mozzarella cheese into 16 small cubes. Take a large teaspoonful of beef mixture and form it into a ball around each cube of cheese.

Heat the oil in a large covered pan, add the meat balls to the pan, cook until brown on all sides.

Add the onion to the pan, cook for 2 to 3 minutes, then add the tomatoes and juice from the can. Bring up to simmering point, cover and cook for 30 minutes.

Uncover pan and cook for a further 10 minutes to allow the sauce to reduce and thicken slightly.

While the meat balls are cooking, cook the spaghetti in boiling salted water for about 10 minutes.

Drain well, then divide among four warmed plates. Taste the sauce and adjust seasoning, divide among the plates of spaghetti then sprinkle the plates with the reserved parsley.

Preparation time 20 minutes
Cooking time 45 minutes
Serves 4

NOODLE AND SEAFOOD CASSEROLE

6 oz (175 g) noodles
salt and freshly ground black
  pepper
½ cup (3 oz, 75 g) frozen peas
1 onion, chopped
1 cup (5 oz, 150 g) fresh, canned
  or frozen crab
1 cup (6 oz, 175 g) peeled shrimp
  (prawns)
8 oz (250 g) can water chestnuts,
  drained
½ cup (4 fl oz, 125 ml)
  mayonnaise
½ cup (4 fl oz, 125 ml) tomato
  juice
½ cup (4 fl oz, 125 ml) fish stock
¼ cup (1 oz, 25 g) cheddar cheese,
  grated
¼ cup (1 oz, 25 g) flaked almonds

Cook the noodles in boiling salted water for 5 minutes, add the peas and onion to the pan and cook for a further 3 minutes.

Drain then put into a large bowl. Add the crab, prawns and water chestnuts.

Mix together the mayonnaise, tomato juice and stock, pour into the bowl, season to taste and mix well.

Transfer the mixture to an ovenproof casserole.

Mix together the cheese and almonds, sprinkle over the top of the casserole.

Cook in a preheated oven 375°F (190°C, Gas mark 5) for 35 to 40 minutes until topping is crisp and browned.

Preparation time 15 minutes
Cooking time 45 to 50 minutes
Serves 4

Watchpoint: If preparing this casserole in advance let the noodles stand until cold before adding the fish.

PAGLIA E FIENO WITH GREEN SPRING VEGETABLES

6 oz (175 g) thin asparagus
4 oz (125 g) fine French beans
6 oz (175 g) broccoli florets
4 oz (125 g) mange-tout (snow peas)
8 oz (250 g) zucchini (courgettes), ends removed and cut into thick sticks
½ cup (4 fl oz, 125 ml) crème fraîche
2 teaspoons cornstarch (cornflour)
salt and freshly ground black pepper
1 lb (500 g) fresh paglia e fieno (any pasta which mixes white and green strands)
freshly grated parmesan cheese

Put the asparagus, beans and broccoli into a pan of boiling water, cook for 3 minutes, add the mange-tout and zucchini and cook for a further 3 minutes. Reserve 1 cup (8 fl oz, 250 ml) cooking water then drain the vegetables.

Mix the crème fraîche with the cornstarch, then add to the reserved cooking water. Put into the pan and heat gently stirring constantly until thickened. Season to taste, then replace vegetables.

Cook pasta in lightly salted water for about 5 minutes. Drain, then transfer to a warmed serving dish. Arrange the vegetables on top of the pasta and serve sprinkled with the parmesan cheese.

Preparation time 10 minutes
Cooking time 15 minutes
Serves 4

PASTA AND VEGETABLE STIR-FRY

12 oz (350 g) tortiglioni
salt and freshly ground black
pepper
3 oz (75 g) sugar-snap peas
(mange-tout or snow peas)
with ends removed
6 oz (175 g) broccoli florets
4 oz (125 g) whole baby corn
1 large carrot, sliced
1 large onion, sliced
2 cloves garlic, crushed
1 large red bell pepper (capsicum),
sliced
1 tablespoon sunflower oil
1 oz (25 g) sunflower margarine
2 tablespoons freshly grated
parmesan cheese

Cook pasta in boiling salted water for 5 minutes, add peas, broccoli, corn and carrot to pan, cook for a further 5 minutes.

Cook onion, garlic and red bell pepper in oil and margarine in a large pan or wok until soft.

Drain the pasta and vegetables, add to the pan, stir briskly until well mixed and heated through.

Divide among four warmed plates and serve sprinkled with parmesan cheese.

Preparation time 10 minutes
Cooking time 15 minutes
Serves 4

Variation: For a meat meal, omit the broccoli but add 6 oz (175 g) thinly sliced beef steak with the onion and garlic.

PASTA NESTS WITH POACHED EGGS

14 oz (400 g) fresh tagliatelle
salt and freshly ground black
pepper
6 slices streaky bacon, rinded and
chopped
4 eggs
1 oz (25 g) butter
2 tablespoons chopped fresh
parsley
½ cup (2 oz, 50 g) cheddar cheese,
grated

Cook the tagliatelle in lightly salted water for about 5 minutes.

Lightly broil (grill) the bacon and lightly poach the eggs.

Drain the tagliatelle, toss with the butter and parsley then divide among four warmed individual ovenproof dishes, making a depression in the center of each one.

Put a poached egg into the center of each tagliatelle nest, season with salt and pepper.

Divide the bacon and cheese among each dish, then broil (grill) until cheese is bubbling. Serve immediately.

Preparation time 10 minutes
Cooking time 10 minutes
Serves 4

Variation: Sliced, cooked sausages could be used instead of the bacon in this recipe.

PASTA PEPERONATA

2 tablespoons olive oil
1 onion, finely chopped
1 clove garlic, crushed
1 large red bell pepper (capsicum),
    thickly sliced
1 large yellow bell pepper
    (capsicum), thickly sliced
1 large green bell pepper
    (capsicum), thickly sliced
8 oz (250 g) tomatoes, skinned and
    chopped
salt and freshly ground black
    pepper
12 oz (350 g) penne
⅓ cup (2 oz) pitted black olives

Heat oil in a large pan, add the onion, garlic and bell peppers, stir around until peppers being to soften.

Add tomatoes, salt and pepper to the pan, stir well, then simmer uncovered for 10 minutes.

Cook penne in boiling salted water for 8 to 10 minutes. Drain well then divide among four warmed plates.

Add the olives to the pepper sauce then spoon sauce onto the pasta.

Preparation time 10 minutes
Cooking time 15 minutes
Serves 4

Advance preparation: The pepper sauce may be prepared 1 day in advance. Keep covered and chilled and reheat gently before serving.

PASTA POMODORO

1 onion, chopped
2 cloves garlic, crushed
1 medium carrot, grated
2 sticks celery, finely chopped
1 tablespoon olive oil
½ cup (4 fl oz, 125 ml) dry white
    wine
1½ lb (750 g) ripe tomatoes,
    peeled and chopped
2 tablespoons tomato paste (purée)
½ teaspoon sugar
salt and freshly ground black
    pepper
3 tablespoons chopped fresh
    parsley
1 lb (500 g) spaghetti

Cook the onion, garlic, carrot and celery in oil in a large lidded pan until soft. Add the wine and boil until reduced to half.

Add the tomatoes, tomato paste, sugar, salt and pepper. Bring to the boil, reduce heat, cook uncovered for about 30 minutes, stirring occasionally, adding a little water if the sauce becomes too dry. Stir in the parsley.

Cook the spaghetti in boiling salted water for 10 minutes. Drain then divide among four warmed plates. Serve with the tomato sauce.

Preparation time 15 minutes
Cooking time 35 minutes
Serves 4

PASTA-STUFFED TOMATOES

1 small onion, chopped
1 small green bell pepper
(capsicum), chopped
2 teaspoons vegetable oil
½ cup (4 oz, 125 g) canned
sweetcorn
6 oz (175 g) cooked rice-shaped
pasta
4 large beef-steak tomatoes
salt and freshly ground black
pepper
¼ cup (1 oz, 25 g) edam or gouda
cheese, finely grated
2 teaspoons tomato paste (purée)
1 cup (8 fl oz, 250 ml) boiling
water

Soften the onion and bell pepper in oil in a pan, transfer to a bowl, then add the sweetcorn and pasta.

Cut a slice from the stalk ends of the tomatoes, and finely chop. Scoop out the tomato pulp, discard the seeds, then add the tomato pulp and chopped tomato flesh to the bowl, season with salt and pepper.

Put the tomato shells into a shallow ovenproof dish, divide the pasta mixture among the tomato shells, then sprinkle with the cheese.

Mix together the tomato paste and water. Pour into the dish. Cook in a preheated oven 375°F (190°C, Gas mark 5) for 20 to 25 minutes, or microwave 5 to 6 minutes on HIGH.

Preparation time 15 minutes
Cooking time 25 to 30 minutes
Serves 4

Microwave tip: If cooking this dish in the microwave, finish off under the broiler (grill) to brown the cheese.

PASTA WHEELS
WITH CHICKEN LIVERS

12 oz (350 g) pasta wheels
salt and freshly ground black
*   pepper*
1 lb (500 g) chicken livers
2 scallions (green onions, shallots),
*   finely chopped*
1 tablespoon vegetable oil
8 oz (250 g) button mushrooms
4 slices streaky bacon, rinded and
*   chopped*
2 tablespoons madeira wine
½ cup (4 fl oz, 125 ml) chicken
*   stock*
1 teaspoon cornstarch (cornflour)

Cook pasta in boiling salted water for about 10 minutes.

Trim and wash the chicken livers, dry well on paper towels.

Soften the scallions in oil, then add the chicken livers, mushrooms and bacon, stir constantly for 2 to 3 minutes.

Add madeira to the pan, bring to the boil. Mix the chicken stock with the cornstarch, add to the pan. Stir constantly until mixture thickens then cook for a further 5 minutes.

Drain pasta and divide among four warmed plates. Taste sauce and adjust seasoning, divide among plates of pasta.

Preparation time 10 minutes
Cooking time 10 minutes
Serves 4

Variation: Substitute port or dry sherry if the madeira is unavailable. The sauce could also be made with thin strips of lambs' or calves' liver.

PASTA WITH FOUR CHEESES

7 oz (200 g) lasagne verde
1 oz (25 g) butter or margarine
2 oz (50 g) flour
2¹/₂ cups (1 pint, 600 ml)
*   skimmed milk*
salt and freshly ground black
*   pepper*
³/₄ cup (3 oz, 75 g) smoked cheese,
*   grated*
³/₄ cup (3 oz, 75 g) emmental
*   cheese, grated*
1 cup (4 oz, 125 g) mozzarella
*   cheese, grated*
¹/₂ cup (2 oz, 50 g) parmesan
*   cheese, finely grated*

Cook lasagne in boiling water for about 5 minutes until just tender.

Drain, then lay out onto paper towels until cool enough to handle.

Melt butter in a pan, add flour, cook for 1 minute, then gradually add the milk, stirring constantly until boiling. Reduce heat and simmer for 2 to 3 minutes, season with salt and pepper.

Mix together the smoked cheese, emmental, mozzarella and half the parmesan cheese.

In a shallow oven proof dish, make layers of sauce, lasagne and cheese, ending with a layer of sauce. Sprinkle with the reserve parmesan cheese.

Cook in a preheated oven (350°F, 180°C, Gas mark 4) for about 40 minutes until golden brown, or microwave for 8 to 10 minutes on high.

Preparation time is 15 minutes
Cooking time 50 minutes
(10 minutes using the microwave)
Serves 4

Microwave tip: If cooking this dish in the microwave, finish off under the grill to brown the top.

PINEAPPLE AND PASTA HAM ROLLS

4 oz (125 g) cooked elbow
   macaroni
1 cup (6 oz, 175 g) canned crushed
   pineapple
1 large pickled cucumber, chopped
½ cup (2 oz, 50 g) edam or gouda
   cheese, grated
1 tablespoon mayonnaise
1 tablespoon pineapple juice
salt and freshly ground black
   pepper
8 slices cooked ham
16 cherry tomatoes

Mix together the macaroni, pineapple, pickled cucumber and cheese in a bowl.

Combine the mayonnaise and pineapple juice, season with salt and pepper. Add to the bowl and mix well.

Divide the macaroni mixture among the ham slices. Roll up and secure with a toothpick (cocktail stick) if necessary.

Put a cherry tomato into each end of the ham rolls.

Preparation time 10 minutes
Serves 4

Note: This is a good recipe for using up leftover macaroni or other pasta shapes.

PINEAPPLE PASTA MERINGUE

1 lb (500 g) can pineapple cubes
  in syrup
milk
3 tablespoons cornstarch
  (cornflour)
3 eggs, separated
4 oz (125 g) cooked pasta rings
⅔ cup (5 oz, 150 g) superfine
  (caster) sugar

Drain the syrup from the can of pineapple and reserve it. Make the syrup up to 2 cups (¾ pint, 450 ml) with milk.

Mix a little of the syrup with the cornstarch to make a smooth paste, add it to the remaining syrup and milk mixture, then put it into a pan, bring to the boil, stirring constantly until mixture thickens then cook for a further 2 to 3 minutes.

Pour sauce into a bowl, then add the pineapple cubes, egg yolks, pasta rings and 1 heaped tablespoon sugar. Mix well then transfer to a deep ovenproof dish.

Beat the egg whites until stiff, lightly fold in the remaining sugar, then pile the meringue over the pineapple mixture.

Cook in a preheated oven 300°F (150°C, Gas mark 2) for about 30 minutes until the meringue is crisp and browned. Serve hot or cold.

Preparation time 20 minutes
Cooking time 35 minutes
Serves 4 to 6

Variation: Any other small pasta shapes could be used instead of the pasta rings.

PIPE RIGATE WITH CHILI AND PROSCIUTTO SAUCE

1 onion, chopped
1 red chili pepper, seeds removed
  and chopped
1 tablespoon olive oil
2 cups (¾ pint, 500 ml) passata
½ teaspoon sugar
1 teaspoon dried oregano
salt and freshly ground black
  pepper
1 lb (500 g) pipe rigate or other
  dried pasta shapes
3 oz (75 g) prosciutto (Parma
  ham)

Cook the onion and chili in the olive oil for 2 to 3 minutes. Add the passata, sugar, oregano, salt and pepper, simmer uncovered for 10 minutes.

Cook the pasta in boiling salted water for about 10 minutes. Drain well then put into a warmed serving dish.

Add the prosciutto to the sauce, pour sauce over the pasta, mix gently together, serve at once.

Preparation time 10 minutes
Cooking time 15 minutes
Serves 4

RAVIOLI WITH RED PEPPER SAUCE

1 onion, chopped
1 clove garlic, crushed
1 tablespoon olive oil
1½ lb (750 g) red bell peppers
  (capsicums), chopped
½ cup (4 fl oz, 125 ml) vegetable
  stock
salt and freshly ground black
  pepper
1 lb (500 g) fresh meat-filled
  ravioli
freshly grated parmesan cheese

Cook onion and garlic in oil in a large pan until soft, but not browned. Add bell peppers, stock, salt and pepper.

Bring to the boil, cover the pan, reduce heat and simmer for about 15 minutes until bell peppers are quite soft.

Put the pepper mixture into a blender or food processor and blend until smooth.

Strain (sieve) the pepper sauce to remove any pieces of pepper skin.

Cook ravioli in boiling salted water for about 8 minutes or according to packet instructions.

Reheat the pepper sauce, if necessary. Divide among four warmed plates.

Drain the ravioli then arrange on top of the pepper sauce. Serve sprinkled with parmesan cheese.

Preparation time 15 minutes
Cooking time 20 minutes
Serves 4

Variation: This sauce could also be served with other filled pastas such as tortellini, or try making the sauce with yellow or orange bell peppers.

Rigatoni with Sweet and Sour Vegetables

12 oz (350 g) rigatoni
salt and freshly ground black
  pepper
2 tablespoons vegetable oil
1 clove garlic, crushed
2 large leeks, cut into thin strips
2 large carrots, cut into thin strips
1 large red bell pepper (capsicum),
  cut into thin strips
4 sticks celery, cut into thin strips
½ cup (4 fl oz, 125 ml) vegetable
  stock
2 tablespoons light soy sauce
2 tablespoons lemon juice
1 tablespoon clear honey
1 teaspoon cornstarch (cornflour)
bunch scallions (green onions,
  spring onions), chopped

Cook the pasta in boiling salted water for 10 to 12 minutes.

Heat the oil in a large pan and sauté the garlic, leeks, carrots, bell pepper and celery.

Mix together the stock, soy sauce, lemon juice, honey and cornstarch. Add to the pan, bring to the boil stirring constantly. Cook for a further 3 to 5 minutes. The vegetables should remain quite crisp. Taste and adjust seasoning.

Drain pasta and divide among 4 warmed plates. Divide vegetables among the pasta. Serve sprinkled with scallions.

Preparation time 15 minutes
Cooking time 10 to 12 minutes
Serves 4

Health tip: If cooking the vegetables in a non-stick pan, you can reduce the amount of oil to 1 tablespoon.

SHERRIED CHICKEN AND FETTUCINI CASSEROLE

8 oz (250 g) fettucini
1 onion, chopped
1 large red bell pepper (capsicum),
*   sliced*
8 oz (250 g) mushrooms, sliced
1 oz (25 g) butter or low fat
*   margarine*
1½ oz (40 g) flour
2 cups (¾ pint, 500 ml) chicken
*   stock*
½ cup (4 fl oz, 125 ml) dry sherry
salt and freshly ground black
*   pepper*
12 oz (350 g) cooked chicken,
*   chopped*
2 tablespoons light (single) cream
½ cup (2 oz, 50 g) cheddar cheese,
*   finely grated*

Cook fettucini in boiling water for 8 to 10 minutes, until still quite firm, then drain well.

Cook onion, bell pepper and mushrooms in butter until soft. Add the flour, cook for 1 minute, then add the stock, sherry, salt and pepper. Bring to the boil, stirring constantly, then cook for 2 to 3 minutes.

Mix together the pasta, chicken, cream and vegetable sauce. Pour into a shallow ovenproof casserole, sprinkle with the cheese. Cook in a preheated oven 375°F (190°C, Gas mark 5) for 30 to 35 minutes, or microwave 8 to 10 minutes on HIGH.

Preparation time 20 minutes
Cooking time 40 to 45 minutes
Serves 4

Microwave tip: If cooking this dish in the microwave, finish off under the broiler (griller) to brown the cheese.

Note: This is an ideal dish for using up the remains of a cooked chicken. Use the chicken carcass to make the stock.

Microwave tip: If cooking this dish in the microwave, finish off under the broiler (grill) to brown the cheese.

SHRIMP WITH PERNOD AND PASTA

12 oz (350 g) orecchieto
salt and freshly ground black
    pepper
1 large head Florence fennel
1 tablespoon olive oil
2 scallions (shallots), finely
    chopped
½ cup (4 fl oz, 125 ml) fish stock
1 teaspoon cornstarch (cornflour)
12 oz (350 g) peeled shrimp
    (prawns)
1–2 tablespoons pernod

Cook the pasta in boiling salted water for 8 to 10 minutes.

Slice the fennel, reserve and chop any green leaves.

Heat oil in a pan, add the fennel and scallions and cook until soft.

Add the fish stock to the pan. Mix cornstarch with 1 tablespoon water and add to the pan. Bring to the boil, stirring constantly until sauce thickens.

Add shrimp to the pan, simmer gently until shrimp are heated through. Add the pernod, taste and adjust seasoning.

Drain the pasta, divide among four warmed plates. Spoon the sauce over the pasta, then sprinkle with the reserved fennel leaves.

Preparation time 10 minutes
Cooking time 10 minutes
Serves 4

SMOKED FISH AND PASTA SALAD

8 oz (250 g) conchiglie
2 tablespoons vegetable oil
1 tablespoon lemon juice
½ teaspoon mild curry powder
3 eggs, hard-cooked
8 oz (250 g) smoked haddock,
    cooked and flaked
bunch scallions (green onions,
    spring onions), chopped
1 cup (6 oz, 175 g) canned
    sweetcorn kernels
salt and freshly ground black
    pepper
2 tablespoons chopped fresh
    parsley

Cook the pasta in boiling water for about 10 minutes. Drain well, transfer to a large bowl.

Mix together the oil, lemon juice and curry powder. Add to the bowl, mix well, let stand until cold.

Halve the eggs, put the yolks to one side, chop the whites.

Add the egg whites, fish, scallions and sweetcorn to the cooled pasta, season to taste and mix well.

Transfer the salad to a serving dish. Strain (sieve) the reserved egg yolks. Mix with the parsley then sprinkle over the top of the salad.

Preparation time 15 minutes, plus standing time
Cooking time 10 minutes
Serves 4

Variation: Other smoked fish could be used instead of haddock. Try using cod, trout or mackerel.

Advance preparation: This salad can be prepared up to 1 day in advance. Keep covered in the refrigerator but bring to room temperature to serve.

SPAGHETTI CASSEROLE

1 onion, chopped
1 lb (500 g) lean ground (minced)
    beef
2 teaspoons olive oil
2 tablespoons tomato paste (purée)
1¼ cups (½ pint, 300 ml) beef
    stock
½ teaspoon dried marjoram
salt and freshly ground black
    pepper
1 oz (25 g) butter
1½ oz (40 g) flour
2 cups (¾ pint, 500 ml) milk
½ cup (2 oz, 50 g) cheddar cheese,
    grated
8 oz (250 g) spaghetti
1 tablespoon grated parmesan
    cheese

Cook onion and beef in oil until beef is no longer pink. Add the tomato paste, stock, marjoram, salt and pepper. Bring to the boil, reduce heat, simmer uncovered for 30 minutes, stirring occasionally, then transfer to a deep ovenproof casserole.

Melt the butter in a pan, add flour, cook for 1 minute, then add milk gradually, stirring constantly until boiling. Cook for 2 to 3 minutes. Remove from the heat, stir in the cheddar cheese.

Cook spaghetti in boiling salted water for about 8 minutes. Drain, then add to the cheese sauce.

Spread the spaghetti over the meat sauce. Sprinkle with the parmesan cheese. Cook in a preheated oven 350°F (180°C, Gas mark 4) for 35 to 40 minutes, or microwave 8 to 10 minutes on HIGH.

Preparation time 15 minutes
Cooking time 1 hour 10 minutes
Serves 4

Advance preparation: All the separate parts of the casserole can be prepared in advance to be assembled just before baking.
Health tip: Skimmed milk and low fat cheese will reduce the fat content in this dish.
Note: If cooking this dish in the microwave, finish off under the broiler (griller) to brown the top.

SPAGHETTINI WITH MUSSELS

2 lb (1 kg) fresh mussels
12 oz (350 g) spaghettini
1 onion, finely chopped
2 cloves garlic, crushed
1 tablespoon olive oil
grated rind and juice of 1 lemon
½ cup (4 fl oz, 125 ml) dry white
* wine*
½ cup (4 fl oz, 125 ml) fish stock
salt and freshly ground black
* pepper*
3 tablespoons chopped fresh
* parsley*

Scrub the mussels well and remove any beards. Rinse in cold water. Put in a large pan with cold water, cover the pan, bring to the boil, cook for 5 minutes shaking the pan from time to time. Drain mussels and put into a large bowl, discarding any mussels that do not open.

Cook the spaghettini in boiling water for 5 minutes, drain and add to mussels.

Soften the onion and garlic in oil then add to the bowl containing the mussels and spaghettini, along with the lemon rind and juice, wine, stock, salt, pepper and parsley. Mix well then divide the mixture among four large wax (greaseproof) paper bags, sealing the bags with metal ties.

Lay the bags on a large baking sheet, cook in a preheated oven 425°F (220°C, Gas mark 7) for 10 minutes.

Transfer the bags to warmed plates. Split open the bags at the table.

Preparation time 15 minutes
Cooking time 15 minutes
Serves 4

Variation: If fresh mussels are unavailable, use canned or bottled mussels or clams.

SPINACH AND PASTA TIMBALES

*2 lb (1 kg) fresh Swiss chard
    (spinach), washed
butter or margarine, for greasing
12 oz (350 g) cooked pastini
1 cup (8 oz, 250 g) low fat soft
    cheese
pinch grated nutmeg
½ cup (2 oz, 50 g) pine nuts
salt and freshly ground black
    pepper
2 eggs, beaten*

Put ¼ of the Swiss chard (spinach) leaves into a bowl, cover with boiling water, let stand for 5 minutes then drain well. Chop the remaining leaves, cook until soft then drain well.

Lightly grease 8 large ramekin or cup molds, approximately 1 cup (8 fl oz, 250 ml) capacity. Line the ramekins with the blanched leaves.

Mix the cooked Swiss chard (spinach) with the pastini, soft cheese, nutmeg and pine nuts, season with salt and pepper, then beat in the eggs.

Divide the mixture among the ramekins. Cover each one with foil then cook in a preheated oven 200°C (400°F, Gas mark 6) for about 30 minutes.

Turn out onto warmed plates to serve.

*Preparation time 15 minutes
Cooking time 35 minutes
Serves 4*

STUFFED PASTA SHELLS

20–24 giant pasta shells
salt and freshly ground black
    pepper
4 oz (125 g) sun-dried tomatoes in
    oil
5 oz (150 g) mild soft goat cheese
5 oz (150 g) low fat soft cheese
2 teaspoons chopped fresh basil or
    1 teaspoon dried basil
1 egg yolk
1 tablespoon freshly grated
    parmesan cheese

Cook the pasta shells in boiling salted water for 10 to 12 minutes, drain then cool under running cold water.

Drain the sun-dried tomatoes reserving a little of the oil.

Finely chop the tomatoes then put into a bowl with the goat cheese, soft cheese, basil, salt, pepper and egg yolk. Mix well then fill the pasta shells with the mixture.

Lay the shells in an even layer in a shallow ovenproof dish. Brush each one with a little of the reserved oil. Sprinkle with the parmesan cheese.

Cover the dish with foil then cook in a preheated oven 400°F (200°C, Gas mark 6) for 20 to 25 minutes, until heated through, or cover dish with microwave-safe plastic wrap (cling film) pierced in a few places then microwave 5 to 6 minutes on HIGH.

Preparation time 15 minutes
Cooking time 30 to 35 minutes
Serves 4

TAGLIATELLE
WITH SMOKED SALMON

1 lb (500 g) green fresh tagliatelle
salt and freshly ground black
    pepper
4–6 oz (125–175 g) smoked salmon
    cut into thin strips
⅔ cup (¼ pint, 150 ml) sour
    cream
1 tablespoon chopped fresh dill
lemon wedges and dill sprigs

Cook the tagliatelle in lightly salted boiling water for about 5 minutes. Drain well then return to the pan with smoked salmon, sour cream, dill and black pepper.

Heat gently, stirring constantly until salmon and cream are just heated through.

Transfer to a warmed serving dish. Garnish with lemon wedges and dill sprigs.

Preparation time 5 minutes
Cooking time 10 minutes
Serves 4

Variation: Boned and flaked fresh or canned salmon could be used instead of smoked salmon.

THREE-MUSHROOM PASTA

12 oz (350 g) amori
½ oz (15 g) butter
1 tablespoon vegetable oil
1 small onion, chopped
2 cloves garlic, crushed
8 oz (250 g) field mushrooms,
  sliced
5 oz (150 g) oyster mushrooms
15 oz (425 g) can Chinese straw
  mushrooms, drained
2 tablespoons oyster sauce
salt and freshly ground black
  pepper
2 tablespoons chopped fresh
  parsley

Cook the pasta in boiling water for about 10 minutes.

Melt the butter and oil together in a large non-stick pan.
Soften the onion and garlic, add the mushrooms and stir
for 2 to 3 minutes.

Drain the pasta, add to the pan with the oyster sauce,
mix well, then taste and adjust seasoning.

Divide among four warmed plates. Serve sprinkled with
the chopped parsley.

Preparation time 10 minutes
Cooking time 15 minutes
Serves 4

Variation: Other varieties of mushrooms could be used,
as available, such as shii-take or wild mushrooms when
in season.

TORTELLINI WITH HAM AND PETITS POIS

1 onion, finely chopped
½ oz (15 g) butter
½ oz (15 g) flour
1¼ cups (½ pint, 300 ml) milk
4 oz (125 g) lean cooked ham, cut into thin strips
¾ cup (4 oz, 125 g) petits pois (tiny peas)
1 tablespoon parmesan cheese
1 lb (500 g) fresh cheese-filled tortellini
salt and freshly ground black pepper
2 tablespoons chopped fresh parsley

Cook onion in butter until soft, add flour, cook for 1 minute then gradually add the milk, bring to the boil, stirring constantly.

Add ham, petits pois and parmesan cheese. Simmer gently for 10 minutes.

Cook tortellini in boiling salted water for 8 minutes or according to the packet instructions.

Drain then divide among four warmed plates. Taste sauce and adjust seasoning.

Pour the sauce over the tortellini, then sprinkle with the chopped parsley.

Preparation time 10 minutes
Cooking time 10 minutes
Serves 4

Health tip: Skimmed milk may be used to reduce the fat content in this dish.

Tortellini with
Hot Cheese Fondue

1 lb (500 g) fresh tortellini
2 cups (8 oz, 250 g) gruyère or
emmenthal cheese, grated
1 clove garlic, crushed
½ cup (4 fl oz, 125 ml)
mayonnaise
½ cup (4 fl oz, 125 ml) dry white
wine
salt and freshly ground black
pepper

Cook tortellini in boiling water for about 10 minutes.

Put the cheese, garlic, mayonnaise, wine, salt and pepper into a small non-stick pan. Heat very gently, stirring constantly until cheese has melted and a thick sauce has formed.

Drain the tortellini, then divide among four warmed plates.

Divide the cheese fondue among individual ramekin dishes. Serve one with each plate of tortellini.

Dip the tortellini into the cheese fondue to eat.

Preparation time 10 minutes
Cooking time 10 minutes
Serves 4

Note: The fondue is best made with a commercial brand of mayonnaise from a jar. The fondue could also be prepared in a fondue pan and served from the center of the table. For a special occasion a little kirsch could be added.

TRENETTE TAPENADE

1 lb (500 g) trenette
7 oz (200 g) can tuna fish, drained
1 clove garlic, crushed
*⅔ cup (3 oz, 75 g) pitted black
  olives*
1 tablespoon capers, drained
*2 oz (50 g) can anchovy fillets,
  drained*
freshly ground black pepper

Cook trenette in boiling water for 8 to 10 minutes.

Put the tuna, garlic, olives, capers, anchovies and black pepper into a blender or food processor and blend to a smooth paste. Add 2 to 3 tablespoons of the pasta cooking water to this tapenade sauce.

Drain the pasta, return it to the pan, stir the sauce into the pasta until the pasta is coated with the sauce. Divide among four warmed plates and serve immediately.

Preparation time 10 minutes
Cooking time 10 minutes
Serves 4

TUNA-STUFFED CANNELLONI

1 cup (8 oz, 250 g) ricotta cheese
7 oz (200 g) can tuna fish, drained
1 bunch scallions (green onions, spring onions), finely chopped
1 small red bell pepper (capsicum), finely chopped
salt and freshly ground black pepper
16–20 quick cooking cannelloni tubes
1¾ lb (800 g) can tomatoes in juice
freshly grated parmesan cheese

Mix together the ricotta cheese, flaked tuna, scallions, red bell pepper, salt and pepper. Divide the mixture among the cannelloni tubes.

Chop the tomatoes into smaller pieces. Put half into a shallow ovenproof casserole. Lay the cannelloni on top, then cover with the remaining tomatoes and juice.

Cover the dish with foil, cook in a preheated oven 375°F (190°C, Gas mark 5) for 35 to 40 minutes until pasta is tender, or microwave about 15 minutes on MEDIUM.

Serve sprinkled with parmesan cheese.

Preparation time 20 minutes
Cooking time 35 to 40 minutes
Serves 4

Health tip: To reduce the fat content, use tuna fish that has been canned in brine.

VANILLA PASTA CREAMS

3 eggs
¼ cup (2 oz, 50 g) vanilla sugar
1¼ cups (½ pint, 300 ml) milk
⅔ cup (¼ pint, 150 ml) light
*   (single) cream*
4 oz (125 g) cooked rice-shaped
*   pasta*
14 oz (400 g) can apricots in syrup

Put disks of non-stick silicone paper into the base of six small ramekin dishes.

Beat together the eggs and sugar. Heat the milk and cream together, then pour onto the eggs and mix well. Stir in the pasta.

Divide the mixture among the ramekin dishes. Put the dishes into a baking pan half-filled with boiling water. Cook in a preheated oven 325°F (170°C, Gas mark 3) for about 35 minutes until set. Remove from the oven, let stand until cold.

Put the canned apricots into a blender or food processor with 3 tablespoons of syrup from the can. Blend until a smooth sauce is formed.

Turn the pasta creams out onto six small individual plates. Remove the silicone paper and serve with the apricot sauce.

Preparation time 15 minutes plus standing time
Cooking time 35 minutes
Serves 6

Variation: Any other fruit could be used for the sauce. For a special occasion add a little brandy or rum.

Note: If vanilla sugar is not available use ½ teaspoon pure vanilla extract (essence) with superfine (caster) sugar.

VERMICELLI AND HAM SOUFFLÉ

1 oz (25 g) cornstarch (cornflour)
2 cups (¾ pint, 500 ml) milk
6 oz (175 g) cooked vermicelli
4 oz (125 g) cooked ham, diced
4 eggs, separated
¼ cup (1 oz, 25 g) gruyère cheese,
*   grated*
¼ cup (1 oz, 25 g) parmesan
*   cheese, grated*
salt and freshly ground black
*   pepper*
butter or oil for greasing

Mix the cornstarch with a little of the milk. Heat remaining milk in a pan until just simmering. Pour onto the cornstarch, mix well then return to the pan. Bring to the boil, stirring constantly, then cook for 2 to 3 minutes.

Transfer sauce to a large bowl, add vermicelli, ham and cheeses. Beat in the egg yolks, one at a time, then season to taste.

In a separate bowl, beat the egg whites until stiff, then lightly fold into the sauce.

Transfer the mixture to a lightly greased 6 cup (2½ pint, 1½ liter) soufflé dish.

Cook in a preheated oven 425°F (220°C, Gas mark 7) for 35 to 40 minutes.

Serve immediately.

Preparation time 15 minutes
Cooking time 40 to 45 minutes
Serves 4

Health tip: Use skimmed milk instead of whole (full-cream) milk to reduce the fat content of this soufflé.

Variation: If a milder flavor is preferred substitute all cheddar cheese for the gruyère and parmesan cheeses.

WHOLEWHEAT CONCHIGLIE WITH BLUE CHEESE AND WALNUTS

1 lb (500 g) wholewheat conchiglie
4 oz (125 g) blue cheese such as gorgonzola or dolcelatte, crumbled
1/2 cup (4 oz, 125 g) mascarpone cheese
1 oz (25 g) freshly grated parmesan cheese
salt and freshly ground black pepper
1/2 cup (2 oz, 50 g) walnuts, chopped and toasted

Cook the pasta in boiling water for 10 minutes. Drain into a colander.

Put the blue cheese, mascarpone and parmesan into the pan, heat gently, stirring constantly until the cheeses have melted. Taste and adjust seasoning.

Return the pasta to the pan, stir around until coated with the cheese sauce.

Transfer to a warmed serving dish and sprinkle with the toasted walnuts.

Preparation time 10 minutes
Cooking time 15 minutes
Serves 4

Fresh, Home-made Pasta

2¼ cups (9 oz, 250 g) strong bread
  flour
1 teaspoon salt
3 small eggs, beaten
1 tablespoon olive oil

Sift the flour and salt into a bowl, add the eggs and oil, mix together until the eggs and flour are incorporated, then transfer to a floured board and knead well until a smooth paste is formed. Wrap the pasta in plastic wrap (cling film) and let stand for 30 minutes.

Cut the pasta into six even-sized pieces, flatten each one out slightly, then feed the pieces through a pasta rolling machine, starting at the widest setting, then reducing the width of the rollers until the pasta is the desired thickness.

Either roll up the pasta and cut into the desired width with a sharp knife or feed the pasta through a pasta cutting attachment. Lay the pasta out onto a clean dish (tea) towel and let stand for 30 minutes to dry out slightly.

Cook the pasta in boiling salted water for 3 to 5 minutes.

Preparation time 20 minutes plus standing time
Cooking time 3 to 5 minutes
Serves 4

INDEX